The Melody of the Woodcutter and the King

AN ACCOUNT OF AN AWAKENING

William Samuel

SEED CENTER

Palo Alto, California

Original paperback first printing, 1976
Copyright © 1976 by William Samuel
All rights reserved.
Calligraphy by Abby Seixas
Joyfully published by Seed Center
Box 591, Palo Alto, California 94302
Made in the United States of America
ISBN 0-916108-08-2

NOTE TO THE READER

Many hymns, chants, prayers and mantras have come down to us through the centuries. We know that certain of them contain an especial and mysterious authority when read aloud. Behind their words, beyond their words—indeed, being their words—lies a Message understood by the Heart alone, simply awaiting our conscious recognition.

THE MELODY OF THE WOODCUTTER AND THE KING is a rhythmic, alliterative mantra of awakening. The significance of its message can lift the laden, world weary seeker of Truth from a distorted sense of the world and himself into a new universe of Peace, All-rightness and childlike Joy unending!

Reader, you may prove this for yourself immediately. For just a time, sit easy like a child and listen to the melody and changing rhythm of this short and simple story. With a tender touch—and without struggling to understand every meaning*—read THE MELODY OF THE WOODCUTTER AND THE KING to yourself aloud. The Heart of you, the Child of you, the Real of you will understand whatever the intellect does not.*

Do not be surprised at the expansion of Awareness, Joy and dominion that are certain to follow soon in your experience.

—William Samuel

Woodsong
1976

PROLOGUE

There is a story to tell
but I am the only one here to tell it
and the only one to listen.
There is a picture to paint
but I am the only one here
with canvas and oil,
the only one who will see it.
There is a symphony to play
yet there is only one here
to draw the bow.
This *one, the Alone One,*
is the only one here to listen.

This is as it should be, however,
for it allows the picture to be painted,
the symphony sounded
and the story told as it truly is.
Then, if there seems an angry word
in the telling,
my Listening will never hear it.
If there seems a distorted scene,
the Seeing I am will understand it,
because one alone is here to listen
to the symphony on this page.
This one, the Only One,
understands His melody!

THE MEETING

Atop my Holy Mountain, I looked up and out;
scepter in hand, I looked roundabout
and beheld a magnificent land, a happy land,
a finished land of harmony.

Thought I,
    This land is my Kingdom
    and I am the King thereof.
    In it I reign.
    In it I command and it is done.
    In it I decree with absolute authority
    and illusion yields itself to me,
    rendering reports of majesty and harmony,

of tender beauty and simplicity.
Then I looked down, unseen.

At the forest's edge
a woodcutter stood chopping with his axe.
Stroke after stroke he fought the forest
and his axe glistened in the sun.

Father, how long must I labor?
I heard him shout.
How long must I contend?
How long before I see Thee face to face,
before I put aside this axe
and take Thy scepter in its place?
How long before I see your abundance,
free to feast forever?

Then the woodman fell to his knees to rest.
Clutching the axe, he whispered,

> *Father, show me what to do!*
> *Show me how to stop this struggle*
> *and still the fear within!*
> *Show me how to quench the come and go,*
> *the ebb and flow between serenity and sadness.*
> *Show me love again, and laughter.*
> *Let discord cease*
> *that I may feel Peace.*
> *Father, there is no worth in* me!
> *Show me Thyself. Show me* Thee!

Oh! Those words of agony I had heard before.
The woodcutter's anguish
had been my own song of yore.

Yea, this man is my Son.
I have found the Prince!
Let me greet him; let me comfort him.
Let me quench his thirst
and take away his axe.
Let me remind him of his dominion
and show him the land of his heritage.
This is my Son in whom I am well pleased.
It is my joy to give him the Kingdom!

From out the brightness of the morning sun
I spoke to him.

> ***I know thee who thou art.***
> ***I am the one you asked for.***

And he knew me as I knew him.

Division was discarded.
We were one again!

Put away your axe,
I told him.
Rest beneath the tree.
Listen to the soft sound
that only comes from me.

Once I cut wood as you, dear Son.
My hands were calloused too—
torn by tribulation and toil,
insufficiency and strife;
but that was long ago as time goes,
long, long ago.
Now I see a universe

too beautiful to hurt
and much too lovely to labor.
Now I see a land
filled with love and laughter.
Now I see children
smiling in the sunshine,
laughing in the Light,
because the Kingdom I speak of
is a land without hunger,
without labor and without strife.
It is a land where no one cries,
where fear is merely foolish fantasy
and where the shadow of death is swept aside
by the Light of understanding.
*This land is **my** land.*
I am the King thereof.

In it I reign
and illusion's reign is ended!

Now that I have found you,
dear heir to my throne,
let me show you this Kingdom
which is your Kingdom too
so you may reign as I.

Come,
I persuaded.
There is no cause to be weary
and heavy laden forever.
The Heaven I speak of is not far away
but close at hand;
you merely perceive it not.

The way there is a sweet way
without bramble or stumbling block
and there is no devil's army
to contend with along the way
nor a single night
to dwell in the wilderness.

Beloved, for only a little while
shall we remember this measured moment
that has a phantom felling oaks,
knowing nothing of Identity.

Slowly the woodman lifted himself from the earth
and we walked thenceforth together.
Down a narrow pathway strewn with flowers
we walked arm in arm.

At length he asked me,
*   What do you mean when you say*
*   that your story is my story too?*

Reader, listen to the song I sing in answer,
for soon you will sound the same symphony
to yourself, even as NOW I sing this measure
to Myself alone.

THE KING'S STORY

Once I cut wood with a borrowed axe
and cleared my kindling from leased acres too.
For me, just as you,
each day was another sashay to battle,
another time to contend,
another wonder what good or evil
would appear before the sunset.
And, just as you, my woodman,
I could not comfort the weary
for echoing their agony.

Oh, there were brief moments of respite
in meditation's frightened fortress,
but I could not SEE the joy

that was 'round about
and the warm tears that love shed
too often turned bitter.

In the moments of greatest agony
a wise man came
from the darkest depths of the forest
to tell me things of comfort.
He came with an ointment for my blisters,
a sharpening stone for my axe;
and while he was with me
I put the blade aside
to hear him tell of good and evil,
of life and death,
of the Messiah, mankind and rest.
Yes, we dreamt dreams together
in the soft, sweet shade of the oak

but when he left—when he left—
I lifted the axe again.
The borrowed blade had been lighter
much too short a time.

Then another wise one came to me
just as he came to you.
He taught that the world is an illusion,
a dreamer's dream of mortality.
   "You are sleeping,"
said he,
   "dreaming all the agony."

   "Then, if this is a dream,"
I answered,
   "awaken *me!*
   My children must eat, dream or not.

I know no other way to feed them;
I can find no easier lot."
But he could not awaken me
and I felled another tree.

Finally a third sage came,
trying to teach that God
is one's source of supply.
   "Throw away your axe,"
said he.
   "Just Be. Just Be!"
But my children were hungry when he left too
and I cut another tree.

Oh, weary son,
so many came with so much to say
that I asked as you did too,

"Lord,
how do I know whom to listen to
and whom to follow?
Which is the Way to go?
Which way is the way to walk?
First one comes, then another—
a third and a fourth and a fifth,
arguing among themselves,
pointing out their own inaccuracies.
Whom must I follow **now**, Father?
Tell me directly!
Tell me in my heart
so I will understand."

But there was only silence
and in anguish I cried,

"Father, show me Thyself,
that I might know myself and who I am.
Reveal *Thyself*
such that I may see beyond this mist—
this miserable mist—
to touch Thee.
You see, I seek to SEE the pure Principle
and perfect Law that pervades
this atmosphere of consciousness;
yet the seeking brings peace
only with an ebb and flow
like seasons that blow
through oaks still standing to be cut."

Yea, my son,
the countless systems of the sages

merely lightened the load a moment.
Every cordon of kindling collected
cried the need for another, another
and still another.
Finally, just as you,
this simplest prayer I cried,
*   "It is **Peace** I ask for, Father;*
*   Perfection I long to see.*
*   Yet, what I ask for must be*
*   the self-same One that You are*
*   in the action of being Me.*
*   Could the distortion, the misery,*
*   be a sharpening goad,*
*   hastening the recognition*
*   of my honest identity?*
*   Oh, Holy Consciousness,*

come *to me—but more tenderly!*
Lift the veil that hides Thee from me.
It is my own veil,
a vile veil I have woven myself."

Then, *it was, beloved.* **Then** *it was!*
Face to face my Father appeared to me,
exactly as I to you!
Lo . . .
face to face the Comforter stood before me
just as I stand before you now!

Tell me,
the woodman implored.
Tell me of that time!

THE ILLUMINATION

I answered the woodman,

It was in the morning, in the Spring
in the month of planting with birds awing
when the newness of everything
is but an instant away.
I had bent myself down to drink from a pond,
and there, reflected in the water he was—
in my own image and likeness he was—
and nowhere could I see the old self at all
or needed to, or wanted to.

From out the morning Light
the Messiah came to me,

softly, quietly,
with the tender touch of love.
Oh, Grand Light of Truth
that shone 'round about!
Splendor beyond words!
Warmth, wonder,
sweet sounds bathed in gossamer beams
from an expanded Heaven
that included me and mine
and all things exactly as they are;
the immaculately conceived
now effortlessly perceived;
incommunicable language of gentle words,
intimate symphony without sound;
Light of Love
wherein no darkness dwells!

Questions no longer; instead,
a simple basking in the soft New Sound
of the Now that All is.
The has-been and shall-be
were seen for what they are.

Then, even as I to you,
my Father said to me,
   "I am He whom thou hath asked for,
   the One you long to see.
   Thy Father-I-am is the I that I am
   and I show Myself to thee
   face to face—eternally!"
I knew Him too, just as you knew Me.

THE HOLY MOUNTAIN

My son,
I said to the woodman,
     there is a mountain in my kingdom
     from which the universe
     may be surveyed as it really is.
     I will take you there
     as my Father has taken me before.
     From this high place
     the gates of the Heart are flung open,
     the scales drop from the eyes,
     the land is seen in its wholeness
     and the questions that were asked before
     remain silent.

Look! Even now it is before you!
This instant it is here!
Tell me what you see, dear one;
tell me what you hear.

The woodman answered,
 I see a high mountain with many plateaus
 and a great multitude walking up many paths
 that wind long distances toward the top.
 On each path a herald is proclaiming
 his way the only way,
 and on the many plateaus
 are many ministers shouting,
  "Rest here! View this vista,
  the most beautiful of them all!"

Yet there is no happiness there.
They curse each other on the different paths
and stand on every plateau
in condemnation
of those above or below.
On the higher plateaus
I hear judgments of those
whose vision is not as wide,
and from the highest plateaus
come the sermons of those
who decry duality and deny it—
in the day they deny,
but in the night, as I,
they still cut wood in their jungle;
they still search the crevasses
for sustenance;

they still stagger through their thickets
and slash.

Tell me, Father.
Which path must I follow?
On which plateau may I rest?

My son,
I answered the woodman,
   to climb o'er the ground
   from plateau to plateau
   is not the way to go.
   There is no path on the mountain
   that leads all the way to the top
   nor a single place where a woodman
   may let go his axe.

There is no plateau on any slope
where one may stop contending with opposites;
for to climb o'er the ground from goal to goal
creates the original twoness—
a climber and the goal.

Then how, *Counselor?*
the woodman asked.

> *How* can *I climb the mountain?*
> *How may I reach the throne?*

Listen softly,
I said to the woodman,

> **listen gently with the heart.**
> **There is no way there but to BE there.**
> **This** *way soars above the ground,*

above the landmarks, above the plateaus,
swiftly, silently, immediately
on wings of Love.
This *is how I shall take you there, Beloved—*
in an instant
in the twinkling of an eye
on the Wings of the Morning.
Indeed, the Way there is to **be** *there.*
Then need you not at each plateau
proclaim it the goal for all
nor whisper longer of those above
or admonish the ones below.
You see, Love is the Key to the mystery.
Love is the astrolabe of Light.
Love alone sounds the melody
heard at the immortal Height.

*Love is the wing that lifts thee there
and there hands thee thy scepter.
Love has beckoned Me, thy Comforter,
because you and I are One.
You and I are Love.*

*Immediately the measured moment ended
and we stood atop our timeless mountain.*

THE KINGDOM

My son,
I said,
look with Me from this High Place.
With the same eye that beheld the axe
now view the Kingdom!
Look to the East.
The sun has risen!
Look to the West
where morning dew glistens.
North! South! All you see here,
as far as you envision here,
is the Kingdom I give you today!

Now, lift up your eye and see
the simple sparrow there,
the soaring swallow,
the sun, the stars.
Everything you see there—
everything envisioned here—
is your very own.

Now, listen to the sounds, Beloved—
whispering wind, laughing children,
distant notes proclaiming NOW your sabbath.
Sounds, too, are my Kingdom, dear one,
and I give you them **all** *today.*

Next, with the inner eye
look at everything childlikeness allows.

Envision the oceans,
the sands, the multitudes,
fair fields of fragrant flowers,
oaks unsown in future seasons,
distant mountains higher yet than this.
These, too, are yours, my Son!
Yea, all you see here,
as far as you envision here,
is the Kingdom you are this day.

Listen. Listen and hear!
Even **now** *you are the only Awareness*
that views this Holy Place!
All you see is the Selfhood you be!
You are this minute
the Holy Witness of Me.

You have naught left to do
but gird up thy loins
and accept thy rightful Identity!

Now, deck thyself with majesty and excellency!
Array thyself with glory and beauty!
Thine own right hand
holding Truth's Scepter
hath saved thee!
From this moment forth, view all things
from the standpoint of Perfection
because thou alone art the King!
Dominion is given you this day!
Yea I say,
be the single Selfhood and reign!
Reign, *King of all creation.*

THE AWAKENING

The woodman's eyes had been opened before
but now was opened his Heart.
From out that place of knowing
where is no sediment of stagnation,
no darkness of reservation,
no blindness of equivocation,
came forth the honest sounds spoken
only from the pinnacle of the mountain,

    It is true! It is true!
    I am the King!
    I am!
    –the very words I whispered
    as tinkling cymbals from the slopes,

the same sounds I prattled
in pious self-righteousness
from the plateaus,
and droned as far-off dreams
along the pathways of desire—
ah, but spoken finally from
the Mountain that Childlikeness is.

*It is so! I **am** the King!*
I have heard of Thee
by the hearing of the ear
but now it is the Eye that seeth Thee,
oh Mind being Me!
This is MY Kingdom!
My Kingdom is ME!
My very Self I see,

all perfect infinity!
I have never seen a sight
nor heard a sound but my own!
Yea, the people and things I see
are not separate nor apart from Me.
They appeared dimly as an impostor's judgment
of the King's infinity.
The plateaus and paths below
were my woodcutter interpretation of Me.
The woodcutter's role
is but the shadow of Me.
At last, at last, I see
the entire universe has its existence
as this Awareness I be!
Truly, it **has** *been the Father's pleasure*
to give the Kingdom to ME!

Oh, how foolish I have been,
writhing in the role of a woodcutter
unaware of Identity.
I viewed the very Self I am
and judged it; then I named it,
bought it, sold it, fought it,
struggled to secure it,
bowed down before it
and chopped it with an axe—
measured it, weighed it,
entombed it in time,
gave it the Life and Authority
that all the time were Mine!
The borrowed axe was borrowed from Myself!
The acres leased were rented from Myself!
The wood was cut for Me alone!

Every tree in the forest is Mine
and every forest in the land is Thine,
One Awareness being all I am!

Now *I look across the valley and see a tree.*
It is Me, because where do I see it
but in the Awareness I be?
And how? **Seeing** *is being ME!*
The tree is an attribute of Loveliness
Deity knows Itself to be!
Yea, God-Awareness is My activity—
faithful Witness of Harmony,
honest Witness of Simplicity,
eternal Action of Deity.
Indeed, this Now-Awareness is Identity!
The impostor's judgment

had been the impostor's agony.

Woodman, reigning new king,
lifts his scepter to speak,
> *I have sought Truth all my life,*
> *but lo . . .*
> *That that I seek, I AM!*
> *No exterior law roots me evermore*
> *to an effete clay.*
> *No season binds me anymore*
> *to await the day*
> *when worms deprive me of living beauty.*
>
> *I am the King!*
> *I am the Law of my Holy Kingdom!*
> *As I decree so it shall be!*

Exterior law is annuled;
no law exists but God-Me.
Outside is inside;
inside, outside;
above and below, the same.
Having been lifted up, I see
my images lifted likewise
and drawn to me,
understood as I understand God-Self to be.
The Millennium begins
as I understand and acknowledge
the perfection already roundabout!

THE PLEDGE

From this time forth, dear Father-Being-Me,
I will reign with justice and dignity.
I will speak to Myself as the One Authority.
I will command without congresses or councils,
without ministers, magistrates or armies.
To see the world's tribulation cease,
I live the Child's transcendent Peace.
It is the counsel of All-Rightness
I listen to,
*the **finished** Kingdom I see,*
revealing Heaven, right here,
to this Awareness being Me.
*Millennium **now** is my Final Decree!*

EPILOGUE

The story has been told now, reader,
yet only one has listened.
The picture has been painted
but one alone has seen it.
The one who plays this symphony
understands its harmony—
the one who listens to its melody
is the softness of the sound.
Indeed, the one who reads this book aloud
is the One who has written it,
for Deity, its Self-Awareness

and all it perceives
are one perfect Identity.

This is your Melody,
dear woodcutter who is King.
Reign with Childlikeness!
Lift up your Heart and sing!

Other Works on
THE AWARENESS OF REALITY
by William Samuel

A GUIDE TO AWARENESS AND TRANQUILLITY

THE **AWARENESS** *OF* **SELF**-*DISCOVERY*

TWO PLUS TWO EQUALS REALITY

OM OM, RAM RAM
COSMIC TOAST AND HOLY JAM

DEAR YOU AND I, WE ARE I AM
QUOTE THE SHEPHERD TO
THE LAMB